Self-Discipline Mindset:
Master Mental Toughness and
Learn Self Control to Achieve
Your Goals

ONUR SERBETCI

DEDICATION

"This book is dedicated to my family, who have always supported me in my journey to financial freedom. Your love and encouragement have been my greatest source of strength."

Copyright

OVERVIEW

"Self-Discipline Mindset: Master Mental Toughness and Learn Self Control to Achieve Your Goals" is a book that provides practical guidance and techniques to help individuals develop self-discipline and mental toughness. The book is divided into ten chapters, every focusing on a different aspect of these two important traits. In this book you will be provided with in-depth understanding of self-discipline, including its definition, benefits, and common barriers to developing it to exploring how to build self-discipline, including setting goals, developing good habits and routines, avoiding distractions, and staying motivated and providing tips for improving mental toughness.

TABLE OF CONTENTS

•Career and work
•Relationships
•Physical and mental health

•Monitoring progress and adjusting your approach
•Staying motivated and accountable
•Continuously learning and growing

•Profiles of successful individuals and their self-discipline habits
•Case studies of individuals who have overcome challenges with self-discipline
•Inspirational stories of self-discipline in action

•Recap of key points and main takeaways
•Encouragement to apply the principles of self-discipline and mental toughness in your own life
•Final thoughts and suggestions for further reading

Introduction to Self-Discipline and Mental Toughness

Self-discipline and mental toughness are qualities that defy easy definition yet are extremely valuable in the pursuit of success and fulfillment in life. Self-discipline can be defined as the capability of exerting control over a person's ideas, emotions, and behaviors in order to achieve a goal that is significant to the individual. One definition of mental toughness is the capacity to continue and triumph in the face of difficulties, stress, and adversity.

Success in many aspects of life, such as personal relationships, professional efforts, academic successes, and both mental and physical toughness, requires self-discipline and mental toughness. The development of these qualities gives individuals the capability to create and realize goals, fully handle stress, and overcome barriers and setbacks with poise and resilience.

This book examines the concepts of self-discipline and mental toughness from both a theoretical and practical standpoint, with the goal of enhancing the reader's understanding of the complexities of these two concepts. The definition, advantages, and drawbacks of self-discipline will be examined in the next chapters, in addition to the strategies for achieving and maintaining it. In addition, the book will explore the idea of mental toughness, exploring both the challenges that may obstruct it and the strategies for fostering and bolstering it.

The book will also look at the practical applications of self-discipline and mental toughness, demonstrating how they can be applied to various aspects of life such as personal relationships, job goals, academic success, and physical and mental health. The final half of the book will provide advice on how to maintain your self-discipline and mental toughness, as well as ideas for more reading and opportunities for introspection.

Self-discipline and mental toughness are not intrinsic qualities that an individual is born with; rather, they are talents that may be honed and developed through time via persistent effort and practice. This is a key aspect to remember because these qualities are not natural qualities that an individual is born with. The journey toward developing self-discipline and mental toughness may be challenging at times; yet, the rewards and benefits that may be obtained make the effort more than worthwhile.

Self-discipline is critical to your personal growth and development, as well as the achievement of your professional and personal goals. Self-discipline is an essential component. It takes a strong will, a deep commitment to one's goals, the capability of delayed gratification, and the ability to resist distractions and temptations. Self-discipline has several benefits, including increased motivation and focus, better time management, better decision-making, and a sense of control over one's life.

On the other hand, mental toughness is a vital component of resiliency and the ability to triumph over challenges and barriers. It requires a strong and positive thinking, as well as the capability to control your thoughts, feelings, and behaviors when faced with adversity. Some of the advantages of mental toughness include reduced stress and anxiety, more self-assurance and self-esteem, and a greater ability to face and overcome challenges and setbacks.

This book delves into the complexities of self-discipline and mental toughness, exploring their interconnected concepts and providing practical strategies and tips for developing and improving these qualities. This book will help you become a more mentally strong and self-disciplined individual, whether your goal is to improve your personal or professional life or simply to become more self-disciplined.

Self-discipline and mental toughness are qualities that are immensely useful in the pursuit of success and achieving fulfillment in life. By gaining a deeper grasp of these ideas and how they apply, people can achieve more success and fulfillment, as well as live more fulfilling and joyful lives.

Image by vectorjuice on Freepik

Understanding Self-Discipline

Self-discipline is a vital ability that allows individuals to control their thoughts, emotions, and actions in order to achieve their goals. Even in the face of distractions, temptations, and obstacles, it entails setting priorities, making intentional choices, and adhering to a timetable and routine. Self-discipline development requires a strong will and a profound commitment to persons objectives, as well as the ability to defer gratification and remain focused on the end goal.

Willpower and motivation are only two aspects of self-discipline. It is about building a set of habits and routines that support your goals and aspirations, as well as the ability to keep to those habits and routines, even in the face of obstacles, temptations, and distractions. This requires self-awareness, introspection, and a thorough comprehension of your motivations and impulses.

There are various and diverse benefits of self-discipline. It gives individuals greater motivation and focus, better time management, better decision-making, and a sense of control over their life. Individuals can break free from the restraints of impulsiveness, procrastination, and distraction by exercising self-discipline and directing their energy and attention toward the things that are most important to them.

In addition, self-discipline is essential for success in many areas of life, such as personal relationships, career aspirations, academic achievements, and physical and mental health. Individuals can attain a higher degree of productivity and success, as well as a greater sense of satisfaction and fulfillment in their endeavors, by setting and adhering to clear goals and routines.

Individuals with high degrees of self-discipline, for example, are more likely to stick to a consistent exercise plan, which can improve physical health and fitness. They are also more likely to pursue their academic and career goals with greater determination and focus, as well as to experience a greater sense of accomplishment and satisfaction in doing so.

Despite its numerous benefits, self-discipline can be difficult to develop and maintain. A lack of motivation is a typical impediment to self-discipline, which can result from a lack of clarity about your goals, a lack of purpose, or a lack of enthusiasm in the activities or tasks at hand. The existence of distractions, temptations, and obstacles is another typical barrier that might damage your ability to remain focused and dedicated to a goal.

It is essential to adopt a proactive and intentional approach to the development of self-discipline in order to overcome these obstacles. This may entail establishing a clear understanding of your goals, values, and priorities and then aligning your thoughts, emotions, and actions with these. The use of a sledgehammer to open a can of worms.

Establishing clear limits and routines is one technique to create an environment that promotes self-discipline. Setting aside particular time for activities such as exercise, reading, or meditation, and making these activities a regular and non-negotiable part of your daily routine, for example, can help to cultivate a greater sense of control over your thoughts, emotions, and actions. Individuals can develop a foundation for self-discipline by doing so, which will lessen the influence of distractions and temptations.

Adopting a growth mindset, where self-discipline is viewed as a skill that can be developed and improved over time, is another strategy for building self-discipline. This requires a willingness to experiment, try new techniques, and learn from failures and setbacks.

In addition to these strategies, individuals can employ a variety of techniques and instruments to cultivate self-discipline and overcome typical obstacles. Mindfulness techniques, such as meditation and journaling, can help individuals become more aware of their thoughts and emotions, as well as develop greater control over their reactions to stress and distraction.

10

Another powerful method for increasing self-discipline is goal setting. Individuals can cultivate a greater sense of focus and motivation, as well as stay motivated and on track toward their goals, by setting clear, quantifiable, and achievable goals. In addition, breaking down larger goals into smaller, more achievable tasks might help individuals overcome procrastination and make greater progress toward their goals.

Last but not least, it's important to realize that developing self-discipline takes time. Rather, it necessitates continual effort and dedication, and persevere requires individuals to be patient, persistent, and willing to persevere through challenges and setbacks. Individuals can make steady progress toward their goals and experience the numerous benefits of this important attribute by approaching self-discipline with a positive and growth-oriented mindset.

Understanding self-discipline is essential for achieving success in numerous areas of life, as well as personal growth and fulfillment. Individuals can cultivate self-discipline, overcome common barriers, and attain a greater level of control over their thoughts, emotions, and actions by growing self-awareness, creating a supportive environment, and using successful strategies and techniques.

"With self-discipline most anything is possible." --Theodore Roosevelt.

III. The Science of Self-Discipline

Self-control is a strong force that can change our life and assist us in achieving our objectives. It is the capacity to restrain our urges, postpone gratification, and concentrate on long-term outcomes. The psychology and neuroscience behind this crucial quality are examined by the science of self-discipline.

The Psychology of Self-Discipline:

The development of self-discipline is influenced by a number of important aspects, which psychologists have long been researching. Self-awareness, or the capacity to keep an eye on our own thoughts, feelings, and behaviors, is among the most crucial. We might start to create plans for combating our own inclinations toward impulsivity or procrastination by becoming aware of them.

Self-regulation, or the capacity to manage our own behavior, is another crucial element. This entails establishing specific objectives, developing plans to achieve them, and holding ourselves responsible for our deeds. It also entails controlling our own feelings, such as boredom or frustration, which might impair our self-control.

The desire to work toward our objectives, or motivation, is a third aspect. When we have a strong sense of purpose or a compelling motivation to accomplish our goals, we are more likely to be self-disciplined. This drive to achieve may come from within, as in a personal goal, or it may come from without, as in the urge to live up to others' expectations.

The Neuroscience of Willpower:

Recent advances in neuroscience have provided insight into the neural processes underlying self-control. One of the major discoveries is that self-control depends on the prefrontal cortex, the area of the brain that controls impulses, decision-making, and planning. Stress, exhaustion, and other conditions have been shown to affect this part of the brain in a way that can make it less effective.

Prefrontal cortex activity has been found to increase in those who are very self-disciplined, and research has also indicated that practice and training can enhance this part of the brain. For instance, it has been demonstrated that mindfulness meditation enhances prefrontal brain function and increases self-control.

One more important discovery is that willpower is a finite resource that might run out over time. This implies that the more self-discipline we exercise, the more difficult it is to keep it up. But, studies have also shown that rest and relaxation, as well as taking part in fun or rewarding activities, can help us regain our willpower.

How Self-Discipline Impacts the Brain and Behavior:

Self-discipline has a profound impact on both the brain and behavior. When we exercise self-discipline, we are strengthening the prefrontal cortex and other areas of the brain that are involved in decision-making and planning. This can help us become more effective at achieving our goals and making better choices in all areas of life.

Self-discipline also has a positive impact on our behavior. It allows us to resist temptation and avoid impulsive or destructive behaviors. It also enables us to focus on long-term results, rather than short-term gratification, which is a key factor in achieving success in any area of life.

The science of self-discipline provides valuable insights into how this important trait works, and how we can cultivate it in our own lives. By understanding the psychology and neuroscience of self-discipline, we can develop effective strategies for building this essential skill, and achieving our goals in all areas of life.

IV. Building Self-Discipline

Self-discipline is the foundation of success. Without it, even the most well-thought-out plans and ideas run the risk of failing. Self-discipline can be defined as the capacity to exert mental, emotional, and behavioral control over oneself in order to accomplish your objectives. It takes concentration, perseverance, and a determination to succeed in order to accomplish it. In this chapter, we will discuss the most important aspects of developing self-discipline, such as establishing goals, making a plan of action, forming positive habits and routines, avoiding distractions and temptations, and maintaining motivation and perseverance.

Setting Goals and Creating a Plan of Action

The first thing to do in order to develop self-discipline is to set goals that are both specific and attainable. Setting goals not only gives you something to work for, but also gives you a feeling of direction in your life. When you work toward your goals, they assist you in maintaining your concentration and keep you motivated. It is essential to ensure that the objectives you set are explicit, quantifiable, attainable, relevant, and time-bound when you are in the process of setting them (SMART). This indicates that your objectives must to be defined precisely, be capable of being measured, be attainable, be in accordance with your values and priorities, and have a target date for completion. One example of a SMART goal would be to replace the phrase "I want to be healthier" with "I want to lose 10 pounds in the next six months by following a healthy diet and exercising frequently." This would be a more specific and measurable objective.

After you have decided what you want to do, the next step is to design a strategy for achieving those goals. You might think of this as a road map that will lead you to the accomplishment of your objectives. It should include a detailed guide that walks you through each step of what you need to do in order to accomplish your objectives. For instance, if your objective is to reduce your weight by ten pounds, your plan of action might involve developing a weekly meal plan, locating a gym or training routine to adhere to, and keeping track of your progress. It is essential to be realistic and honest with oneself on the goals that one can actually accomplish in their lifetime.

Goal Setting

S   Specific

M   Measurable

A   Attainable

R   Realistic

T   Time-bound

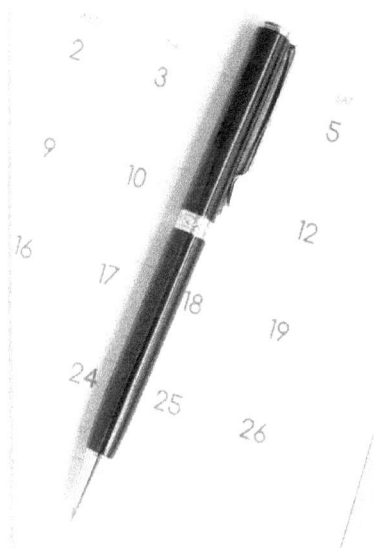

Developing Good Habits and Routines

Good habits and routines are the cornerstones of self-discipline. They help you build momentum and make progress toward your goals. When you establish good habits, you take the guesswork out of decision-making, reducing the amount of mental energy required to make progress. This leaves you free to focus on other important tasks and areas of your life.

One of the most effective ways to build good habits is to make them a part of your daily routine. For example, if you want to become a more disciplined person, you might start by waking up at the same time every day, doing a daily workout, or journaling for 10 minutes each day. Over time, these habits will become automatic and second nature, freeing up mental energy and allowing you to focus on other areas of your life.

"We are what we repeatedly do. Excellence then is not an act, but a habit." --Aristotle

Avoiding Distractions and Temptations

Distractions and temptations are major roadblocks to self-discipline. They can take many many forms, such as social media, television, junk food, or procrastination. To avoid these distractions, it's critical to understand what causes them and devise ways for dealing with them.

One useful method is to create a distraction-free atmosphere to eliminate distractions. Turning off your phone, closing your office door, or finding a quiet spot to work are all examples of this. Another option is to better organize your time so that you can avoid distractions and temptations during your most productive periods. For example, if you are most productive in the mornings, make sure you use that time to work on your most critical duties rather than checking email or social media.

Staying Motivated and Persistent

One of the most important aspects of developing self-discipline is remaining motivated and persistent. Without desire and persistence, no matter how well you plan and execute your routine, you are likely to fail in your self-discipline activities.

Finding meaning and purpose in what you do is an important strategy to stay motivated. This includes comprehending why you are pursuing a specific objective and how it corresponds with your values and beliefs. When you have a clear sense of purpose, it is easier to stay motivated and strive toward your goals even when obstacles appear.

Having a growth mentality is another crucial aspect in remaining motivated. This entails viewing setbacks and challenges as chances for growth and learning rather than failures. You are more likely to confront problems with determination and resilience when you have a growth mindset, which can help you stay motivated and persistent in the long run.

It is also critical to recognize and celebrate tiny accomplishments along the way. This can help you stay motivated and feel a sense of progress and success, which can feed your enthusiasm to strive towards your goals in the future.

Persistence, in addition to motivation, is essential for developing self-discipline. Perseverance entails sticking to your strategy and habits even when they are unpleasant or challenging. It takes a strong will and desire to succeed, even when times are rough.

Focusing on the process rather than the end is one of the most effective strategies to create tenacity. This entails concentrating on the procedures necessary to reach your objectives rather than merely the ultimate result. By focusing on the process, you may stay motivated and tenacious even when the end result appears far.

Finally, finding support and accountability in your self-discipline path is critical. A support system, such as a friend, family member, or coach, can offer encouragement and help you stay on track with your goals and habits.

Setting goals, formulating a plan of action, forming healthy habits and routines, avoiding distractions and temptations, and remaining motivated and persistent are all necessary steps in achieving self-discipline.

image by KamranAydinov on Freepik

V. Having Good Habits and Being Productive

Making good habits is one of the most efficient strategies to achieve self-discipline. With time, habits, which are automatic behaviors, can either serve us or stand in our way. We are more likely to attain our goals and keep up our self-discipline when we have positive habits that support them. Here are some key steps for building good habits that support self-discipline:

1. **Start Small:** When it comes to building good habits, it's important to start small. Trying to make too many changes at once can be overwhelming and lead to burnout. Instead, pick one habit that you want to develop and focus on that for at least a month before adding another one. This will help you create a sustainable habit and build momentum.

2.   **Identify Triggers:** Every habit has a trigger, which is the cue that sets off the behavior. For example, if you want to develop a habit of going to the gym in the morning, the trigger might be setting out your workout clothes the night before. By identifying the trigger for your desired habit, you can make it easier to follow through.

3.   **Create a Plan:** Having a plan for your habit can be the difference between success and failure. Think about what specific actions you need to take to develop the habit and write them down. This could include scheduling time for the habit, setting reminders, or finding an accountability partner.

4.   **Track Your Progress:** It's important to track your progress when developing a new habit. This can help you stay motivated and see the progress you are making. You could use a habit tracking app, a planner, or simply a piece of paper to mark off each day that you complete the habit.

5.   **Celebrate Your Wins:** Celebrating your wins, no matter how small they may seem, can help keep you motivated and encourage you to keep going. Whether it's treating yourself to a nice meal or giving yourself a pat on the back, taking time to acknowledge your progress can help you stay on track.

6.   **Make it Enjoyable:** Finally, it's important to make your new habit enjoyable. If you don't enjoy the habit, it will be much harder to stick to it. Find ways to make the habit fun, such as listening to music while you do it, or finding a workout buddy to make exercise more social.

By incorporating these steps into your daily routine, you can develop good habits that support your self-discipline. With consistent practice and effort, these habits will become automatic and help you achieve your goals.

How to Become Productive

It's easy to get distracted and put things off, but with the right mindset and strategies, you can learn to be more productive and make better use of your time. Here are some tips that will help you get more done:

Set specific goals and prioritize your tasks:

To stay on track and get things done, you need to know exactly what you want to do and break your goals down into steps you can take. Make a list of things you need to do and put them in order of how important and urgent they are. Start with the hardest or most time-consuming task. When you finish it, you'll feel good about yourself and be more likely to finish the rest of your list.

Manage your time wisely:

Managing your time is a key part of being productive. Make the most of your time by setting aside specific times to work on tasks and getting rid of things that might distract you, like social media or TV. Use a timer or an app to keep you on track and help you manage your time well.

Creating routine:

Setting up a daily routine can help you stay focused and keep going throughout the day. Set a regular time to wake up and go to bed, and plan your day around your goals and priorities. To recharge and prevent burnout, plan breaks.

Get organized:

A messy workspace or schedule can make it hard to get work done. Take the time to clean up your space, whether it's your desk or your computer files. Use tools like calendars or software for managing projects to keep track of dates and times.

Prioritize self-care:

Self-care is essential for being productive. To maintain your physical and mental health, make time for exercise, healthy meals, and quality sleep. You'll have the energy and focus needed to be productive when you prioritize your health.

Focus on one task at a time:

It can be tempting to do more than one thing at once, but doing so can slow you down. Instead, give your full attention to one task at a time. You'll be able to get more done and do better work.

Eliminate distractions:

Social media, emails, and phone calls are all examples of things that can be distracting. Find your biggest distractions and do what you can to get rid of or reduce them. During work hours, turn off notifications or use apps to block websites that are distracting.

Being productive takes discipline and focus, but with the right way of thinking and plans, you can get more done and reach your goals. By having clear goals, managing your time, making a routine, getting organized, putting self-care at the top of your list, focusing on one task at a time, and getting rid of distractions, you can be more productive and live a happier life.

VI. Mental Toughness

In recent years, the idea of mental toughness has been getting more attention, especially in sports and other high-performance activities. The ability to overcome obstacles, stick with difficulties, and stay motivated in the face of difficulty is known as mental toughness. It is essential to success because it helps people stay focused, stay calm under pressure, and keep going even when things get hard.

So, what is mental toughness exactly? Mental toughness is a combination of emotional and psychological toughness, willpower, and determination. It is a way of thinking that lets people stay calm and focused in the face of challenges, setbacks, and obstacles. As it enables individuals to overcome adversity and pursue their goals with tenacity and unwavering resolve, it is an essential component of success.

There are numerous and varied benefits of mental toughness. First of all, having mental toughness helps people stay focused and motivated even when they face challenges and obstacles. This is because mentally tough individuals are less likely to become discouraged and give up on their goals when faced with challenges. No matter what, they are able to maintain their focus, persevere through challenges, and keep moving forward toward their goals.

Individuals with mental toughness are also able to stay calm and collected when they are under a lot of stress. This is especially important in high-pressure situations, where staying calm and collected can mean the difference between success and failure. Individuals are able to think clearly and make decisions that are in their best interests even when they face stress and adversity by maintaining their focus and remaining calm.

Another benefit of mental toughness is that it helps people overcome common problems that often get in the way of success. For example, self-doubt is one of the most common things that can make it difficult to maintain mental toughness. Self-doubt can be very debilitating because it hurts people's confidence and makes it hard for them to pursue their goals with conviction. But mentally tough individuals can overcome self-doubt by focusing on their strengths and staying committed to their goals, even when they feel down or unsure.

Mental toughness is also frequently tested by fear. Individuals can be held back by fear in a variety of ways, making it difficult for them to take chances, go after their dreams, or face challenges head-on. Mentally tough individuals, on the other hand, can overcome fear by facing it head-on, embracing challenges, and learning from their experiences. This gives them the confidence they need to face new challenges and go after their goals with courage and determination.

So, how can individuals increase their mental toughness? The best way to build mental toughness is to adopt a growth mindset and see challenges as opportunities for learning and improvement. This means that you have to learn to see setbacks as chances to grow instead of as reasons to give up. It also means accepting challenges, even difficult ones, and learning from both positive and negative experiences.

Focusing on building resilience is another way to get mentally tough. This means learning how to get back up after adversity, overcome obstacles, and keep your focus and determination in the face of adversity. This can be done by using a combination of positive self-talk, visualization, and mindfulness techniques, as well as by building a strong support network of friends, family, and mentors who can give you encouragement and support when you need it most.

It takes dedication to persons own growth and development to cultivate mental toughness. This means taking the time to think about your life, figure out where you can improve, and work on becoming a better person in all areas. Additionally, it entails being willing to try new things, welcoming change, and constantly looking for new challenges and chances for growth. You'll be better able to handle life's challenges and obstacles and reach your goals with more focus and determination if you have greater mental toughness. To develop mental toughness, you must overcome common challenges like negative self-talk, self-doubt, and putting things off. With practice and persistence, you can build mental toughness and enjoy the many benefits it has to offer.

TIME FOR ACTION

Image by rawpixel.com on Freepik

How to Bust Laziness and Harness the Power of Willpower:

At some point in their lives, everyone is affected by laziness, which is a natural state. It is the tendency to avoid or postpone tasks that we know we should undertake. Procrastination and laziness are the most powerful opponents of self-discipline and productivity, resulting in squandered opportunities and a sense of unfulfillment.

Fortunately, there are numerous methods for combating laziness and harnessing the power of willpower. In this chapter, we'll look at some of the most successful techniques to overcome laziness and increase productivity:

Recognize the root cause of laziness:

The first step in busting laziness is to identify the underlying cause of the problem. Common causes of laziness include lack of motivation, fear of failure, and overwhelm. Once you have identified the root cause of your laziness, you can begin to address it with the right strategy.

Break down big tasks into smaller ones:

At some point in their lives, everyone is affected by laziness, which is a natural state. It is the tendency to avoid or postpone tasks that we know we should undertake. Procrastination and laziness are the most powerful opponents of self-discipline and productivity, resulting in squandered opportunities and a sense of unfulfillment.

Fortunately, there are numerous strategies for combating laziness and harnessing the power of willpower. In this chapter, we'll look at some of the most successful techniques to overcome laziness and increase productivity:

Set clear goals and deadlines:

Set specific goals and deadlines as another helpful strategy for overcoming laziness. This offers you a clear idea of what you need to do and when you need to do it, and it might help you stay motivated to finish the assignment.

Use positive self-talk:

Negative self-talk can be a significant impediment to productivity. Substitute negative ideas with positive affirmations that remind you of your skills and achievements. This might help you overcome self-doubt and drive you to continue pursuing your goals.

Reward yourself:

A powerful incentive might be rewards. After finishing a task or reaching a goal, reward yourself with something you appreciate. This can help to reinforce positive habits and keep you motivated to keep working toward your goals.

Practice willpower exercises:

Willpower is the ability to control impulses and make sound judgments in the face of temptation or distraction. Willpower may be strengthened by practice, much like a muscle. Among the most effective exercises are:

1. **Delaying gratification:** Resist the urge to indulge in something immediately and instead delay the gratification.
2. **Mindful breathing:** Practice deep breathing and focus on the present moment, reducing stress and increasing focus.
3. **Mental rehearsals:** Visualize yourself succeeding in a challenging situation to build confidence and mental fortitude.
4. **Surround yourself with positive influences:** The people you surround yourself with can have a significant impact on your mindset and productivity. Surround yourself with positive, supportive people who encourage and motivate you to stay focused and achieve your goals.

Laziness and lack of willpower can be challenging, but with the right strategies, you can overcome them and achieve your goals.

VII. Improving Mental Toughness

Mental toughness is an important part of personal development, and it is a combination of numerous traits and skills that allow individuals to perform well even in difficult situations. Developing mental toughness necessitates a concerted effort, as well as the development of critical skills and traits that can help individuals face challenges with determination, resilience, and positivity.

Building resilience and bouncing back from setbacks

Resilience, or the capacity to overcome obstacles, setbacks, and defeats, is an important component of mental toughness. When faced with adversity, resilience enables individuals to overcome obstacles and keep making progress toward their goals. The concept that challenges and setbacks are opportunities for development and growth is known as a growth mindset, and it is necessary for the development of resilience. Individuals can learn to view challenges not as reasons to give up but rather as opportunities for growth by adopting a growth mindset.

Focusing on the development of a strong support system that includes friends, family, and other sources of encouragement and support is one method to create resilience. This can be done in a variety of ways, but one of the most effective ways is to build resilience. Even when confronted with setbacks and challenges, this support system can help individuals stay motivated and keep working toward their goals. In addition, individuals can benefit from adopting a routine and structure, which can help them stay on track and focus on their goals, even when they are confronted with difficult circumstances.

"Concentration and mental toughness are the margins of victory." --Bill Russell

Cultivating a growth mindset:

As was mentioned earlier, one of the most important components of developing your mental toughness is creating a growth mindset. A growth mindset is characterized by the notion that abilities and intelligence can be developed by hard work, dedication, and a willingness to learn from mistakes and setbacks. This belief distinguishes a growth mindset from a fixed mindset. This mindset can help individuals overcome challenges and continue to grow and develop as people over the course of their lives.

Mindfulness and self-reflection are two practices that can be used to create a growth mindset. This is setting aside time on a daily basis to reflect on your thoughts, feelings, and behaviors, with the goal of identifying areas in which there is room for growth and change. Mindfulness and self-reflection can help individuals develop a more positive and constructive mindset, as well as help them obtain a deeper awareness of their own strengths and flaws.

Developing a positive attitude and outlook:

Having a positive attitude and outlook is another crucial aspect of improving mental toughness. This involves developing an optimistic and hopeful mindset, and learning to see the best in others and in difficult situations. Developing a positive attitude can help individuals to stay motivated and to overcome challenges, and it can also have a positive impact on their relationships and overall well-being.

One way to develop a positive attitude is to practice gratitude and to focus on the things in life that bring joy and fulfillment. This can involve keeping a gratitude journal, where individuals write down the things they are grateful for each day. It can also involve engaging in activities that bring joy and fulfillment, such as spending time with loved ones, engaging in hobbies and interests, and participating in meaningful work and volunteer opportunities.

Image by macrovector on Freepik

Managing stress and anxiety:

Stress and anxiety are common challenges that can negatively impact mental toughness, and they can also have a negative impact on overall health and well-being. It is important for individuals to develop effective strategies for managing stress and anxiety, and to learn to recognize and respond to the physical, emotional, and cognitive symptoms of stress and anxiety.

One way to manage stress and anxiety is to practice mindfulness and relaxation techniques, such as deep breathing, meditation, and yoga. These techniques can help individuals to reduce stress and anxiety, and to develop a greater sense of calm and well-being. Additionally, engaging in regular physical activity, such as exercise, can also help individuals to manage stress and anxiety, and to improve their overall health and well-being.

Improving mental toughness requires a deliberate and intentional effort, and a deep commitment to self-improvement. With the right tools and strategies in hand, anyone can become mentally tougher and better equipped to navigate the ups and downs of life. Whether you're looking to overcome a personal challenge, perform better at work or school, or simply become a more resilient and emotionally balanced individual, the principles of mental toughness are a great place to start.

By building resilience and learning to bounce back from setbacks, cultivating a growth mindset, developing a positive attitude and outlook, and managing stress and anxiety, you can become a more mentally tough individual. With each small step you take in these areas, you'll find yourself growing stronger, more confident, and better able to handle the challenges that come your way.

So take the first step today, and start building the mental toughness you need to succeed in life. Whether you start small, with a few simple habits, or dive in headfirst, the rewards of a stronger, more resilient mind are endless. With determination and commitment, you can become the best version of yourself, and achieve all the goals you've set for yourself.

VIII. Applying Self-Discipline and Mental Toughness to Different Areas of Life

Self-discipline and mental toughness are essential skills that can be applied in various aspects of life to achieve success and happiness. Whether it be in your personal life, career, relationships, or physical and mental health, these skills can help you overcome challenges and reach your goals. In this chapter, we will explore how to apply self-discipline and mental toughness to different areas of life.

Personal Life

In your personal life, self-discipline and mental toughness can help you achieve your goals and maintain a balanced and fulfilling life. For example, if you want to read more books or take up a new hobby, self-discipline will help you make time for these activities and stick to your plan. Additionally, mental toughness will help you overcome the challenges and obstacles that come your way and keep you motivated to reach your goals.

One way to apply self-discipline in your personal life is by setting priorities and establishing routines. Take time each day to reflect on what is important to you and what you want to achieve. Then, set aside time for these activities in your daily routine. This could be as simple as waking up early to read or taking a walk after dinner. By following a routine, you'll be more likely to stick to your goals and achieve success.

Mental toughness is also important in your personal life. It can help you handle stress and difficult situations in a more positive and productive way. For example, if you're feeling overwhelmed, take a few minutes to reflect on what is causing the stress and what you can do to overcome it. This could be anything from taking deep breaths, to going for a walk, to reaching out to someone for support. By developing mental toughness, you'll be better equipped to handle stress and maintain a healthy and balanced life.

In the workplace, self-discipline and mental toughness can help you achieve success and reach your career goals. For example, self-discipline can help you focus on your work and maintain a positive attitude, even when the work is challenging. Additionally, mental toughness can help you stay motivated and persevere, even when you face obstacles or setbacks.

One way to apply self-discipline in the workplace is by setting achievable goals and creating a plan of action. This could include setting daily, weekly, or monthly goals, and breaking down larger projects into smaller, manageable tasks. Additionally, establish a routine for work and stick to it, even when you face challenges. This could include taking breaks, prioritizing tasks, and focusing on one task at a time.

Mental toughness is also important in the workplace. It can help you handle stress and maintain a positive attitude, even in difficult situations. For example, if you're feeling overwhelmed, take a few minutes to reflect on what is causing the stress and what you can do to overcome it. This could be anything from taking deep breaths, to reaching out to a colleague for support, to going for a walk. By developing mental toughness, you'll be better equipped to handle stress and maintain a positive and productive work environment.

Image by redgreystock on Freepik

Relationships:

In your relationships, self-discipline and mental toughness can help you maintain healthy and fulfilling relationships. For example, self-discipline can help you make time for your relationships and prioritize them in your life. Additionally, mental toughness can help you handle conflicts and challenges in a positive and productive way.

One way to apply self-discipline in your relationships is by setting aside time for your loved ones and making the effort to maintain your relationships. This could be as simple as scheduling a weekly dinner with family or taking the time to practice self-care and prioritize physical and mental health. In terms of relationships, self-discipline and mental toughness can help individuals to communicate effectively, manage conflicts, and maintain healthy boundaries. Furthermore, applying these qualities in the workplace can lead to greater productivity, better time management, and improved work-life balance.

One important aspect to keep in mind when applying self-discipline and mental toughness to different areas of life is to start small and gradually increase the difficulty of your goals and habits. Rome was not built in a day, and it is unrealistic to expect overnight transformations. Instead, focus on making small and consistent progress each day towards your desired outcome.

For example, if you want to improve your physical health, start by incorporating simple habits such as drinking more water, taking short breaks for stretching, or going for a daily walk. As you begin to see progress and develop a sense of accomplishment, you can gradually increase the difficulty of your habits, such as incorporating strength training into your routine or taking up a new sport.

Similarly, when it comes to developing mental toughness, it is important to start by facing small challenges and gradually increasing the difficulty of your challenges. This could involve challenging negative self-talk, learning to manage stress, or practicing mindfulness and self-reflection. As you become more comfortable and confident in your ability to handle challenges, you can begin to tackle bigger and more difficult problems.

Applying self-discipline and mental toughness to different areas of life requires consistent effort, perseverance, and a growth mindset. It is important to start small and gradually increase the difficulty of your habits and goals, and to continuously challenge yourself to grow and develop as an individual. Remember, every small step forward is a step towards greater success, happiness, and fulfillment in all areas of life.

Career and Work

Self-discipline and mental toughness can help you accomplish success and your career goals in the workplace. Self-discipline, for instance, can help you maintain a positive attitude and focus on your work even when it is difficult. Even when you face obstacles or setbacks, mental toughness can help you persevere and stay motivated.

Setting goals that are within your capabilities and developing a strategy for achieving those goals is one method of exercising self-discipline in the workplace. This may involve defining goals on a daily, weekly, or monthly basis, as well as breaking down larger undertakings into a series of smaller, more achievable tasks. In addition, it is important to set a schedule for your work and to remain committed to it regardless of the challenges that you may face. Taking breaks, organizing tasks in terms of priority, and concentrating on only one thing at a time are all examples of this strategy.

In the workplace, mental toughness is equally as important as physical toughness. Even in difficult circumstances, it can help you manage stress and maintain a positive attitude. For instance, if you are feeling overwhelmed, you should take some time to think about what is creating the stress in your life and what you can do to find a way to overcome it. It might be as simple as taking a few deep breaths or as involved as going for a stroll or reaching out for assistance from a coworker. You will be better equipped to handle stress and maintain a positive and productive work atmosphere if you develop mental toughness.

IX. Maintaining Self-Discipline and Mental Toughness

Developing self-discipline and mental toughness is not a one-time task, but an ongoing process. To maintain the habits, routines, and mindset necessary to achieve success, you must monitor your progress, stay motivated and accountable, and continuously learn and grow. This chapter will explore how to maintain self-discipline and mental toughness in your daily life and achieve long-term success.

Monitoring Progress and Adjusting Your Approach

Tracking your progress is essential for preserving self-control and mental toughness. Periodically analyzing your progress will help you identify areas for improvement and make any required changes to your approach. It will also allow you to celebrate your tiny victories and keep you motivated to continue on your path to success.

Setting Specific, Measurable, Achievable, Relevant, and Time-Bound (SMART) Goals is one of the most effective ways to assess your progress. Setting SMART goals gives you a framework to track your progress, identify obstacles, and adapt your strategy. The term "celebration" refers to a celebration of the completion of a project or the publication of a book. It is also important to keep track of your progress. This will allow you to look back on your journey and realize how far you've come.

Staying Motivated and Accountable

Staying motivated and accountable is another critical component of maintaining self-discipline and mental toughness. Without motivation, you are unlikely to maintain your habits and routines, and without accountability, you are unlikely to hold yourself responsible for your actions.

One way to stay motivated is by finding an accountability partner, whether that be a friend, family member or coach. An accountability partner can help you stay on track and provide support when you need it. Additionally, publicly announcing your goals or progress can help keep you motivated and accountable. This can be done through social media, public speaking or simply sharing your journey with friends and family.

Continuously Learning and Growing

Lastly, in order to maintain self-discipline and mental toughness, it is important to consistently study and grow. Learning new skills, enrolling in classes, reading books, and seeking out new experiences can all help you develop new perspectives and ways of thinking, as well as boost your flexibility. When confronted with obstacles, it is important to maintain your mental toughness and resilience. One way to do this is to view failure and mistakes as opportunities for growth.

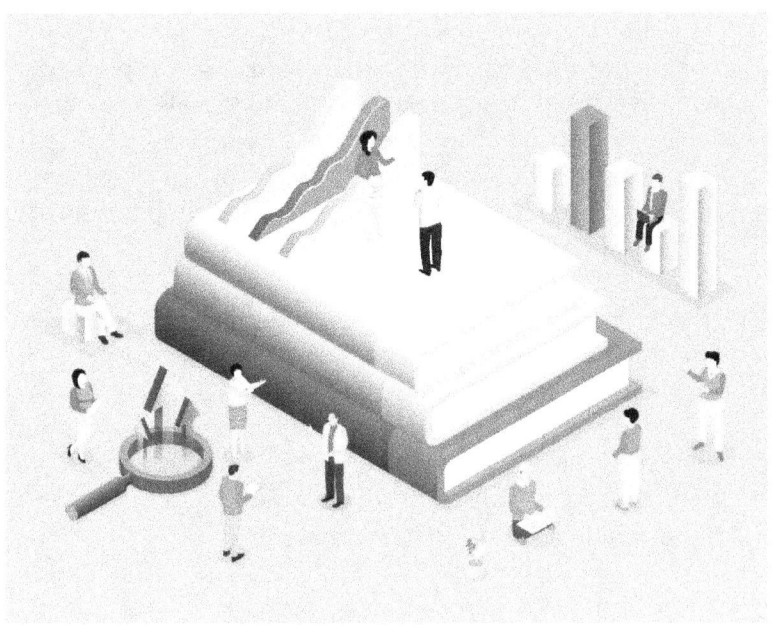

Image by jcomp on Freepik

Seeking out mentors or coaches is a proven method for continuing to learn and grow. In order to help you grow and overcome challenges, these individuals can offer direction, support, and comments. In addition, building relationships with individuals who work in the same profession or industry as you can give you with invaluable insights and viewpoints.

Monitoring your progress and making necessary adjustments to your approach are two important aspects of maintaining self-discipline and mental toughness. To determine what is working and what isn't, you should constantly assess your goals, habits, and routines. It's important to be willing to try new things and adjust your approach if something isn't working.

In order to keep your self-discipline and mental toughness in check, it is essential to keep oneself motivated and accountable. This could include finding someone to hold you accountable or joining a support group that can help you stay on track with your goals. Although this might help to reinforce your motivation and dedication, it is also important to recognize your progress and successes along the way.

Another important aspect of maintaining self-discipline and mental toughness is continuously learning and growing. This might involve reading books, attending seminars or workshops, or working with a coach or mentor. By continuing to learn and grow, you can stay motivated and engaged in your personal and professional development.

In addition to these strategies, it's also important to practice self-care to maintain your mental and emotional well-being. This might involve getting regular exercise, eating a healthy diet, getting enough sleep, and taking time to engage in activities that bring you joy and relaxation.

Maintaining self-discipline and mental toughness is an ongoing process that requires dedication, commitment, and a willingness to adapt and grow. By monitoring your progress, staying motivated and accountable, and continuously learning and growing, you can build the self-discipline and mental toughness you need to succeed in all areas of your life.

Maintaining self-discipline and mental toughness is essential for achieving success in all areas of life. Monitoring your progress, staying motivated and accountable, and continuously learning and growing are all critical components of maintaining these traits. By incorporating these practices into your daily life, you can overcome obstacles, achieve your goals and lead a fulfilling and successful life. Remember, it takes consistent effort and a willingness to adapt and grow to maintain self-discipline and mental toughness, but the rewards are well worth the effort.

X. Real Life Examples of Self-Discipline in Action

When we delve deeper into the world of self-discipline, it's essential to understand that it's not simply an abstract concept to which we strive; it's something we can see and experience in action. Real-life examples of self-discipline in action offer us with motivation and tangible evidence of the importance of this important quality. We can learn how we can implement similar principles in our own lives by examining how self-discipline has positively impacted the lives of successful individuals.

Profiles of successful individuals and their self-discipline habits:

One real-life example of self-discipline in action is the legendary basketball player Kobe Bryant. Known for his extreme work ethic, Kobe would wake up at 4 am every morning to train before anyone else. He also had a strict diet and sleep regimen to maintain his physical and mental health. These habits, coupled with his talent and determination, helped him become one of the greatest basketball players of all time.

Another successful individual who exemplifies self-discipline is Elon Musk, the CEO of SpaceX and Tesla. Musk is known for his intense work ethic and his relentless pursuit of his goals. He often works 80-100 hours per week, has a strict schedule, and is always looking for ways to improve his businesses. His self-discipline has allowed him to achieve tremendous success in multiple industries.

Case studies of individuals who have overcome challenges with self-discipline:

Self-discipline can also help individuals overcome challenges in their lives. One such individual is J.K. Rowling, the author of the Harry Potter series. Before she became a successful writer, Rowling was a struggling single mother living on welfare. Despite her circumstances, she remained focused on her goal of becoming a writer and maintained a strict writing schedule to ensure she made progress every day. Her self-discipline paid off, and she went on to become one of the most successful authors in history. Another example of self-discipline in action is Nick Vujicic, a motivational speaker born without limbs. Despite facing numerous challenges, Vujicic has remained positive and motivated throughout his life, thanks in part to his self-discipline. He has developed a rigorous routine of daily exercise and meditation to maintain his physical and mental health and stay motivated to achieve his goals.

Inspirational stories of self-discipline in action:

There are countless inspirational stories of individuals who have demonstrated self-discipline in extraordinary ways.

One such story is that of Aron Ralston, the hiker who famously cut off his own arm to free himself after becoming trapped under a boulder. Ralston's self-discipline and determination to survive allowed him to make a difficult and life-saving decision in the face of extreme adversity.

Another example is that of David Goggins, a former Navy SEAL and ultra-endurance athlete who overcame childhood trauma and obesity to become one of the toughest men in the world. Goggins credits his success to his unwavering self-discipline, which includes extreme physical training, cold exposure therapy, and mental toughness exercises.

Real-life examples of self-discipline in action demonstrate the power and potential of this crucial trait. By looking to successful individuals, those who have overcome challenges, and those who have demonstrated extraordinary levels of self-discipline, we can gain insight into how we can apply similar principles in our own lives. Whether we're seeking success in our careers, personal lives, or health and wellness, self-discipline is a critical component to achieving our goals and living a fulfilling life.

Conclusion

As we conclude our discussion on self-discipline and mental toughness, it is important to reflect on the key points and takeaways from this guide.

We have discussed the importance of setting goals, creating a plan of action, developing good habits and routines, avoiding distractions and temptations, and staying motivated and persistent in order to build self-discipline. Additionally, we have explored the definition and benefits of mental toughness, common challenges to mental toughness, and strategies for improving mental toughness such as building resilience, cultivating a growth mindset, developing a positive attitude, and managing stress and anxiety.

We have also discussed how to apply these principles to different areas of life such as personal life, career and work, relationships, and physical and mental health. By taking deliberate and intentional action in these areas, we can build the mental fortitude needed to overcome obstacles and achieve our goals.

It is important to remember that building self-discipline and mental toughness is not a one-time event, but an ongoing process. Monitoring progress, adjusting our approach, staying motivated and accountable, and continuously learning and growing are all critical components of maintaining and improving our self-discipline and mental toughness.

In order to maintain and improve our self-discipline and mental toughness, we must monitor our progress towards our goals and be willing to adjust our approach when necessary. This may involve tweaking our routines, changing our goals, or seeking out new resources or support systems.

Staying motivated and accountable is also crucial in maintaining self-discipline and mental toughness. This can involve finding a workout buddy, joining a support group, or hiring a coach or mentor to help keep us on track and motivated. It is important to continuously learn and grow in order to improve our self-discipline and mental toughness. This may involve reading books or articles, attending seminars or workshops, or seeking out new experiences that challenge us and help us to develop our mental fortitude.

In conclusion, developing self-discipline and mental toughness is a lifelong journey that requires deliberate and intentional effort. However, by setting clear goals, developing good habits and routines, avoiding distractions and temptations, staying motivated and persistent, and applying these principles to different areas of life, we can build the mental fortitude needed to overcome obstacles and achieve our goals. So, don't wait any longer, start implementing these principles in your life and reap the benefits of a disciplined and mentally tough mindset.

Image by pch.vector on Freepik

ACKNOWLEDGMENT

I would like to express my deepest gratitude to all of the individuals who have helped and supported me throughout the creation of this book. Special thanks to my family for their unwavering love and encouragement, and to my friends and colleagues for their invaluable feedback and support. I also extend my gratitude to the many authors and researchers whose work inspired me and contributed to the ideas presented in this book.

www.ingramcontent.com/pod-product-compliance
Lightning Source LLC
Chambersburg PA
CBHW071142220526
45467CB00015B/1773